Health Careers in Sports

CAREERS OFF THE FIELD

CAREERS OFF THE FIELD

Health Careers in Sports

By Michael Burgan

Mason Crest

450 Parkway Drive, Suite D
Broomall, PA 19008
www.masoncrest.com

© 2016 by Mason Crest, an imprint of National Highlights, Inc.

Printed and bound in the United States of America.

Series ISBN: 978-1-4222-3264-4
Hardback ISBN: 978-1-4222-3268-2
EBook ISBN: 978-1-4222-8526-8

First printing
1 3 5 7 9 8 6 4 2

Produced by Shoreline Publishing Group LLC
Santa Barbara, California
Editorial Director: James Buckley Jr.
Designer: Bill Madrid
Production: Sandy Gordon
www.shorelinepublishing.com

Library of Congress Cataloging-in-Publication Data is on file with the publisher.

Cover photo: Newscom/Harry Walker/MCT

CONTENTS

Key Icons to Look For

Words to Understand: These words with their easy-to-understand definitions will increase the reader's understanding of the text, while building vocabulary skills.

Sidebars: This boxed material within the main text allows readers to build knowledge, gain insights, explore possibilities, and broaden their perspectives by weaving together additional information to provide realistic and holistic perspectives.

Research Projects: Readers are pointed toward areas of further inquiry connected to each chapter. Suggestions are provided for projects that encourage deeper research and analysis.

Text-Dependent Questions: These questions send the reader back to the text for more careful attention to the evidence presented here.

Series Glossary of Key Terms: This back-of-the-book glossary contains terminology used throughout this series. Words found here increase the reader's ability to read and comprehend higher-level books and articles in this field.

Foreword
By Al Ferrer

So you want to work in sports? Good luck! You've taken a great first step by picking up this volume of CAREERS OFF THE FIELD. I've been around sports professionally—on and off the field, in the front office, and in the classroom—for more than 35 years. My students have gone on to work in all the major sports leagues and for university athletic programs. They've become agents, writers, coaches, and broadcasters. They were just where you are now, and the lessons they learned can help you succeed.

One of the most important things to remember when looking for a job in sports is that being a sports fan is not enough. If you get an interview with a team, and your first sentence is "I'm your biggest fan," that's a kiss of death. They don't want fans, they want pros. Show your experience, show what you know, show how you can contribute.

Another big no-no is to say, "I'll do anything." That makes you a non-professional or a wanna-be. You have to do the research and find out what area is best for your personality and your skills. This book series will be a vital tool for you to do that research, to find out what areas in sports are out there, what kind of people work in them, and where you would best fit in.

And that leads to my third point: Know yourself. Look carefully at your interests and skills. You need to understand what you're good at and how you like to work. If you get energy from being around people, then you don't want to be in a room with a computer because you'll go nuts. You want to be in the action around people, so you might look at sales or marketing or media relations or being an agent. But if you're more comfortable being by yourself, then you look at analysis, research, perhaps the numbers side of scouting or recruiting. So you have to know yourself.

And you have to manage your expectations. There is a lot of money in sports but unless you are a star athlete, you probably won't be making much in your early years.

I'm not trying to be negative, but I want to be realistic. I've loved every minute of my life in sports. If you have a passion for sports and you can bring professionalism and quality work—and you understand your expectations—you can have a great career. But just like the athletes we admire, you have to prepare, you have to work hard, and you have to never, ever quit.

Series consultant Al Ferrer founded the sports management program at the University of California, Santa Barbara, after an award-winning career as a Division I baseball coach. Along with his work as a professor, Ferrer is an advisor to pro and college teams, athletes, and sports businesses.

Introduction

Words To Understand

assessment: the process of determining a situation so that the right next steps can be chosen

diagnostic: relating to a diagnosis, or the process of determining what kind of injury or illness someone has

orthopedics: the branch of medicine that specializes in preventing and correcting problems with bones and muscles

psychologist: a person trained to help others solve mental and emotional problems

As 50,000 cheering fans watch, the quarterback takes the snap and hands off to the fullback. The runner seeks a slice of daylight through the converging bodies of his linemen and the opposing defenders. Finally, the runner is hit, and he goes down—hard. A few seconds pass as he writhes in pain on the field. The crowd falls silent, and a man from the sidelines rushes toward the downed player. He is the team's athletic trainer, the first line of defense in assessing the player's injury and working quickly to fix it.

The trainer has years of education and experience, but he still feels the pressure of the situation. Bob Howard (pictured at left) serves as the head athletic trainer for the University of Connecticut, and he knows firsthand what it's like after he helps an injured athlete off the field. "You have about 30 seconds to focus in on that athlete, maybe a minute," he says, "to really figure out what is going on, and whether they're safe to either go back [into the game] or you have to do a further exam and get them to the doctor." And while the athlete's health is the trainer's top concern, sometimes a coach is looming nearby, encouraging the player to suck it up and get back on the field. The best trainers, though, do what's right for the athlete.

The Importance of Sports Medicine

At the college and professional levels, sports are big business. Fans want to see the best athletes competing in every contest. The athletes train hard to excel at their sport and prepare their bodies for the rigors of competition. But accidents and injuries can take an athlete off the playing field. That's when athletic trainers and a variety of other highly skilled medical professionals step in. They help the injured athletes recover and return to their sport at the same level of performance they had achieved before.

Sports medicine is the general term that includes jobs and careers that help athletes prepare themselves for their sports and help them heal when they're injured. Athletic trainers are probably the sports medicine professionals that most sports fans know, since trainers come on the field to assist athletes during a game. But behind the scenes, athletes also rely on physical therapists (PTs), doctors, and surgeons to take care of their injuries.

In most cases, these health experts work together as a team. After the athletic trainer makes the on-the-field **assessment**, a doctor steps in to examine the injury and decide the treatment plan. Depending on the injury, the doctor might send the injured

Pro teams have trainers and physicians on hand to quickly deal with any injuries that happen in the games.

athlete for **diagnostic** tests such as an X-ray or MRI. A physician examines the results and sets up guidelines for the trainer and PT to follow to help the athlete heal and then return to the playing field in the days or weeks to come.

If necessary, the doctor might refer the athlete to a surgeon. Pro and some college teams have surgeons on staff, who specialize in **orthopedics** and surgical procedures commonly performed on athletes. In 2013, for example, the Super Bowl-champion Seattle Seahawks had four physicians taking care of their players.

With less severe injuries, physical therapists play a major role in determining treatment and measuring an athlete's recovery. At times, if a team does not have its own physical therapists, the trainer might play that role. Or the athletes might go to private PT clinics with staff that specializes in sports medicine.

Away From the Game

For some people interested in sports medicine, their contributions come in a lab, not in the locker room. Doctors and therapists who might not want to regularly treat patients can turn to research positions in sports medicine. That includes studying how the body moves during physical activity and how to improve performance; finding new methods for preventing and treating sports injuries; and studying the effect of physical activity on different parts of the body. Many researchers interested in sports medicine belong to the American College of Sports Medicine (ACSM). The ACSM is dedicated to advancing sports medicine and exercise science. Researchers may not step on the field, but they make important contributions.

Before the Game

Not all the work of athletic trainers, PTs, and other sports medicine professionals takes place after an injury. Nutritionists help athletes eat a proper diet to stay healthy and strong. Other members of the sports medicine team try to ensure that athletes do the proper training, such as lifting weights, exercising, and stretching, to keep them in top shape and hopefully prevent injuries in the first place. And in many sports, a trainer takes time before the game to tape the athletes or prepare braces for players still recovering from an injury.

Sports medicine also goes beyond an athlete's physical well-being. Sometimes athletes, especially younger ones, see the team trainer as someone they can come to with personal problems or ask about health issues not related to their sport. Says UConn's Howard, "You're that trusted medical resource." And for athletes struggling with a loss of confidence or other mental issues, sports **psychologists** are available to help. Dr. Sean Richardson, a leading sports psychologist, summed up the job for the Web site Careers in Psychology: "You're trying to help them deal with things in their life that may be holding them back from achieving higher performance."

No matter what their specific job is, sports medicine experts share two traits: They love sports, and they care about the athletes they treat.

Athletes of all kinds—professional or amateur—can benefit from working with a professional physical therapist to make sure workouts are done risk free.

Words To Understand

accredited: meeting a standard of excellence or skill

clinical: relating to a clinic, or the hands-on study a medical professional does to gain experience before starting a job

internships: jobs, often unpaid, that aspiring professionals take to gain supervised experience

kinesiology: the study of human movement

physiology: the study of living organisms, specifically how cells, organs, and muscles work together

rehabilitation: the treatments used to help someone recover from an injury

Getting Started

From an early age, Leigh Weiss knew he wanted a career in athletics. By high school, though, he realized he didn't have the skills to pursue a pro sports career. That's when he became interested in athletic training, an interest that grew when he was in a car accident and needed months of rehabilitation.

He saw the importance of physical therapy for recovering from an injury and regaining strength. When he went to college, Weiss majored in athletic training. After more study, he landed a job with the New York Giants of the National Football League.

Leigh Weiss's story is typical of many people who enter sports medicine. They combine their love of sports and competition with an interest in medicine. More specifically, they want to see injured athletes regain their top form and excel as they did before.

Starting Early

Many of the jobs within sports medicine require advanced college degrees, meaning at least six years of study after high school. For a physician or sports psychologist, even more schooling is required, and many people in the overall field do extra study or receive certificates in particular areas. Physical therapists, for example, can be certified as strength and conditioning specialists if they want to help athletes develop their strength and build endurance in the best way possible.

But even before entering college, it helps to start thinking about how you can prepare for a job in sports medicine. Keith Steigbigel, a physical therapist who works with both professional

Finding Funds for School

According to the College Board, in 2013–14, the average cost of a four-year college ranged from just over $18,000 to almost $41,000, depending on the kind of school and where it's located. Students interested in studying sports medicine can turn to various sources for financial aid, including scholarships given by different organizations. The National Athletic Trainers Association, for example, awards the Jack Cramer Scholarship, named for a pioneer in the field. The American College of Sports Medicine also gives awards to help students meet the cost of a college education.

and amateur athletes, said that high school students considering the field should take as many science classes as possible—and do well in them. "PT school is challenging and competitive," Steigbigel said, so a commitment to hard work is important. Some physical therapy programs now require high school students to shadow a professional like Steigbigel, so they get a sense of the work and the skills the job requires.

College Choices

All of the different sports medicine jobs share an emphasis on sciences that explore how the body (and sometimes the mind) works. That means taking courses in **physiology**, which is the study of muscles, organs, and cells, and how they work. Another important subject is anatomy, which focuses on the structure of the body. These classes and others help sports medicine experts know what is wrong when athletes are injured. Some of the other subjects examine how the body should move properly (**kinesiology**) and how to provide care for specific injuries.

For each of the four main fields covered in this book, here's a closer look at the academic programs and other requirements you'll need to fulfill before starting your job.

Athletic Trainer

Every state except Alaska has a college or university that offers a four-year (bachelor's degree) program in athletic training. As outlined by the National Athletic Trainers Association (NATA), course work gives students skills in five major areas: injury prevention; **clinical** evaluation and diagnosis; immediate and emergency care; treatment and **rehabilitation**; and organization and professional health and well-being. Not all the learning takes place in a classroom. Students also have to work with actual patients, under the watchful eye of a certified athletic trainer or another health professional.

After receiving a degree from an appropriate school,

Degrees in Sports Medicine/ Exercise Science

The four sports medicine jobs focused on in this book are not the only fields in sports medicine, of course. People looking to combine athletics and health can find jobs in several different fields after earning just a bachelor's degree in sports medicine or exercise science. In many cases, though, the jobs do require some certification. Here's a listing of some of those jobs, provided by the American College of Sports Medicine:

- Aerobics Instructor
- Exercise Specialist in a hospital
- Employee Fitness Director with a business
- Personal Trainer
- Physical Education Teacher

students are eligible to take NATA's Board of Certification exam. Passing that exam allows new athletic trainers to work in most states, but some states call for further licensing or exams. About 70 percent of athletic trainers get a master's degree before starting their careers. Those programs generally require two more years of study. Some athletic trainers, like Leigh Weiss of the Giants, get their four-year degree in athletic training and then pursue a master's in another area. Weiss has a master's in kinesiology, along with a doctorate in physical therapy.

Nearly every career in sports medicine calls for extensive schooling, including at least college and sometimes post-graduate studies.

Students can take other paths to get the college education they need to qualify for certification. Someone with a bachelor's degree in a related field, such as exercise science, can get a second bachelor's in athletic training. Or people with a bachelor's can enter a master's program designed for students who have not already studied athletic training.

Physical Therapist

Physical therapists go through at least six years of education after high school. They must attend schools **accredited** by the Commission on Accreditation in Physical Therapy Education (CAPTE), which is part of the American Physical Therapy Association (APTA). As of 2015, all accredited schools have to offer a doctorate, the degree required to practice physical therapy anywhere in the United States.

The doctorate program usually runs for three years after a student has completed a bachelor's degree. Some schools specify that the bachelor's be in some sort of science. Other schools offer six-year programs that let students do their undergraduate and doctoral studies at the same place. Students who know they want to focus on sports medicine and want more exposure to the field can choose a school that offers a dual athletic training/physical therapy degree. They do their undergraduate work in athletic training and their graduate work in physical therapy. After completing their doctorate, new physical therapists must take exams for a license for the state in which they want to practice.

Newly graduated therapists can pursue jobs or **internships** to specialize in a current area within their field, including orthopedics or sports medicine. For the latter, a student must have completed an athletic training program or received some training in emergency medicine. A residency combines classroom work with more clinical practice. A fellowship does the same, but in an even more intense way, and might focus on just one part of the body, such as the hand or spine.

A physical therapist might use weight machines or other devices to help their patients heal properly.

Sports Doctor/Surgeon

The path to becoming a team doctor or surgeon is the longest of any of the sports medicine professions. In college, students usually take a pre-med curriculum, which focuses on the sciences. The next step is to get into a four-year medical school, which is competitive. In 2013, more than 690,000 students competed for just over 20,000 slots at U.S. medical schools. Excellent undergraduate grades are crucial for getting into med school.

In med school, students do both classroom and clinical work and may have the chance to take some sports medicine courses. Once they pass the exam to become medical doctors, they complete a residency program that focuses on either primary care or surgery. Within primary care, family medicine is a popular residency choice for future sports medicine doctors. There is currently no residency in sports medicine.

More than ever before, sports surgeons can use their skills to get their patients out of the operating room and back to the court or the field.

For a non-surgeon, the next step is a one-to-two year fellowship in sports medicine. Surgeons can do the same, or they can take a fellowship that focuses on a particular body part. After completing the fellowship, a surgeon can operate on athletes. The primary care doctor, however, must also pass a certification exam.

Primary care doctors can still treat sports injuries even if they don't take a sports medicine fellowship, but becoming certified as a sports medicine doctor tells both typical patients and college and pro teams that a doctor has special skills related to athletics.

Sports Psychologist

During college, the potential sports psychologist should take courses in psychology and physical education. Some schools offer a specific sports psychology bachelor's degree, though it's more common to get that training in master's and doctorate programs. The graduate work typically lasts four to six years and can include internships. Students should also take classes that focus on counseling, the one-on-one work psychologists do with patients, as opposed to research. The counseling involves getting clinical experience, which means working with patients under the guidance of a licensed psychologist. Different states have different rules for obtaining a license. States may require up to 6,000 hours of clinical experience before a psychologist can qualify for a license.

Will There Be Jobs?

In general, the health fields are booming in the United States, and the U.S. government expects the number of jobs to increase until at least 2020. Sports medicine, though, can be trickier to enter, depending on the kind of work you want to do. Paid, full-time positions as an athletic trainer, staff PT, or team doctor are limited at the college and professional ranks.

The good news for sports medicine professionals is they have skills that will help non-athletes or the "weekend warriors" who play sports

As long as there are people doing physical activity, there will be a need for medical professionals to help them heal.

in their spare time for fun. Keith Steigbigel sees the emphasis on staying physically active to continue, so physical therapists will have plenty of work treating injuries. In sports psychology, Dr. Sean Richardson told the Careers in Psychology Web site that psychologists learn ways to help all sorts of people improve their performance. He said, "There are a lot of people that want to be the best at something that is not about sports." Those skills provide job opportunities in the business world to balance with working with athletes.

Text-Dependent Questions

1. Name one of the major subjects that sports medicine students will probably study in college.

2. Based on the stats in this chapter, is it easy or hard to fight competition to get into medical school?

3. What type of sports medicine expert works with an athlete on mental health issues?

Research Project

Find out who the sports medicine professionals are at your school and ask them how they got their jobs. At what colleges did they study? What subjects did they cover? Did they ever have internships?

Words To Understand

accelerated: sped up or made to move faster

endorphins: pain-reducing chemicals produced in the brain

ultrasound: a medical therapy that uses sound waves to ease muscle tension and reduce pain

Hard at Work

When the U.S. Olympic team traveled to London for the 2012 Summer Games, Dr. Sean McCann went with them. He and other sports psychologists were there to make sure the Americans competed at a high level against the world's best athletes.

McCann started as a sports psychologist for the United States Olympic Committee 21 years ago, when his field was in its infancy. Back then, he spent time trying to convince teams that sports psychologists could help improve athletic performance. Now, they understand the importance of mental health for athletic achievement.

McCann and his team demonstrate the key role of all sports medicine professionals: preventing medical problems or treating them afterward. But each type of specialty has different methods or tasks to accomplish those goals. Here's a look at some of the realities of the careers in various parts of sports medicine.

Making Movement Happen

Physical therapists make sure injured athletes regain the level of performance they had before their injury. Keith Steigbigel said that PTs are "movement dysfunction specialists." A key part of their job is studying "movement patterns—what is normal movement and what is abnormal movement." Based on their knowledge of such fields as physiology and kinesiology, the therapists know when sports-related physical motions such as throwing, kicking, or running are not right. Their goal, working with the athlete, is to bring the motion back to normal by healing and strengthening an injured body part.

Since few professional teams have full-time PTs, the therapists often do their work

Using Electricity to Heal

Chances are that most people have felt the sharp zing of an electrical shock, even if only from static electricity. From an early age, we learn that electricity can be harmful. But for physical therapists, low levels of electrical current are useful tools. Most PTs use a process called electrical nerve stimulation (TENS) to help control pain. A machine that produces low voltages of electricity is attached to an injured limb with small pads. The electricity curbs pain by blocking the pain signal from the nerves in a damaged area. TENS may also stimulate the brain to release its own natural painkillers, called endorphins. Another useful electrical process is called electrical muscle stimulation (EMS), which helps muscles contract to strengthen them.

A physical therapist's treatment room is filled with gear to help injured bodies heal and move.

in some kind of clinic or hospital. A typical treatment room is an open space with various tables and equipment at different locations. PTs put their patients on the table to examine them and have them do exercises. The equipment can include weight machines, exercise balls, and **ultrasound** machines, which help reduce pain. Other tools for controlling pain and helping muscles heal include hot and cold packs.

When seeing patients, the physical therapists' first step is to assess the movement of the injured body part. They perform tests to determine the range of motion. The therapist moves the limb in all directions, looking to see how well it matches what is the standard range of motion for a healthy limb and how much pain the movement creates. The first step in the treatment process is restoring an athlete's full range of motion.

Once the range of motion is where it should be, the PT focuses on two other key concerns: full strength and full function. Building strength involves a variety of exercises, depending on the body part. Full function means the injured person can do normal activities with ease. But for an athlete, full function means more than just combing his hair or putting on her shoes. For a baseball pitcher, for example, full function means going back to the field and throwing a pitch at 90 miles per hour again. Reaching that level of function requires more rigorous treatment to build strength and flexibility.

On the Field, in the Locker Room

The work of the athletic trainer, the first line of medical defense in sports, can vary greatly. At the high school level, a trainer usually oversees athletes for all home games and may travel with some teams for away games. At the college level, some schools have individual trainers for major sports, while other trainers might be responsible for several sports. At the pro level, one team usually has several trainers.

The major "office" for athletic trainers is the playing field, whether it's a gym used for basketball or a football stadium.

During both practices and games, the trainers are constantly following the action to see if any athlete is hurt. When an injury occurs, the trainers begin their first assessment of the player. Later, the trainers work with a team doctor or general sports doctor to decide if the athlete needs to see a specialist or might require imaging, such as an X-ray or MRI.

Athletic trainers have to go where the athletes go, often working with them before and during games.

Before or after games and practices, athletic trainers have a number of duties. They tape up the players, do last-minute exercises or treatments for players who are still recovering from injuries, and then bring their equipment to the field. Daily activities can vary, depending on the sport.

For Bob Howard, the head trainer of the University of Connecticut football team, the Monday following a Saturday

Bob Howard (blue cap) travels with his football team wherever it goes.

game starts at 6:30 A.M. He and his staff spend the first few hours assessing new injuries and assisting players beginning rehab. They never know exactly what they're going to face: "We could have a week where we don't get anybody hurt or we could have a week where we have 30 new patients or have someone we're scheduling for surgery."

Based on the initial assessment of the players, Howard then meets with the coaches, to let them know the players' availability for practice during the coming week. The athletic trainer, like other sports medicine staff, also spends time writing reports to document the nature of the injury and the treatment plan.

For away games, the athletic trainers for major sports pack up trunks with all the medical supplies they might need on game day, such as bandages, braces, ice packs, splints, and crutches. Then they travel with the team for the event. While teams might go to beautiful cities to play, the trainers have no time for sightseeing. "It's a business trip," Howard said.

At the professional level, the athletic trainers' season doesn't end with the final game. Leigh Weiss, of the New York Giants, told AOL Jobs, "Despite the season only being four to five months out of the year, there is very little down time for athletic trainers in the NFL." They work with team doctors to schedule off-season surgeries and then work with the athletes as they rehab from the surgery. Before the teams draft new players, the trainers are gathering medical information about the players their teams are interested in selecting. Then, several months before the season starts, the trainers work with athletes as they begin their training for the next season.

Ready When Needed

Team doctors or sports doctors in general don't have the constant contact with athletes that athletic trainers do. They usually have jobs at universities or hospitals, while some run their own private practice. Dr. Christopher Ahmad, for example, is the head team physician of the New York Yankees but is also a professor and works at a New York hospital. The team also uses Dr. Daniel Murphy to help injured players. He's based in Tampa, Florida, where the Yankees train and have a minor-league team. For Murphy, a busy time comes when the season ends, as players rehabilitate from injuries. On his practice's Web site he writes, "There's a lot of pressure to get these players healthy and back on the field as soon as possible. It's kind of an **accelerated** rehabilitation program where the stakes are very high, but the players are also very driven and motivated, so it's an exciting process to help them recover from their injuries."

For sports medicine surgeons, their most direct contact with athletes comes in their office or an operating room. They order diagnostic tests, prescribe medicine when necessary, and do surgery

The most common sports surgeries are on the shoulder's rotator cuff or on knee ligaments.

when an injury is severe. Sports surgeons also help plan the rehabilitation process after an injury or surgery.

Keeping the Mind Focused

Most psychologists have an office where they conduct their work. Patients regularly come to see them for an hour session, until the patients feel their particular problems have been solved. Things work a little differently for Sean McCann and other sports psychologists for the Olympic team. They start working with athletes several years before the next Games begin. This long-term work helps the psychologists gain the athletes' trust. That can entail a lot of travel—up to 100 days per year—

as psychologists go with the athletes to training sessions and competitions.

The issues sports psychologists can address are varied. They include helping athletes to:

- **Stay focused during events**
- **Build self-confidence**
- **Improve communication with teammates or coaches**
- **Overcome fear of injury**
- **Reduce anxiety about failing**

The time an athlete spends talking with a trained sports psychologist might just pay off with time spent on the championship podium accepting winning medals.

In many cases, McCann told *Monitor on Psychology*, "It's not so much that there's something going wrong. It's like strength conditioning; it's part of what [athletes] do to get ready for competition season."

The issues aren't always about what's happening on the playing field. Real-life stresses and problems—a divorce, a death in the family—can negatively impact an athlete's performance. The sports psychologist helps with those problems, too. "You can't wait for those issues to resolve themselves," McCann said. "The game schedule is the game schedule; they need to be ready to go."

Each sports medicine specialist performs wherever needed, but all work with the same goal: making sure the athlete is ready, mentally and physically, to do his or her best.

Text-Dependent Questions

1. Name one of the teams mentioned in this chapter that have full-time team doctors.

2. At what college does athletic trainer Bob Howard work?

3. By what process does a TENS device help heal muscles?

Research Project

Look at which kind of injuries or medical conditions are more likely to be examined with an X-ray and which with an MRI. What technology does each use?

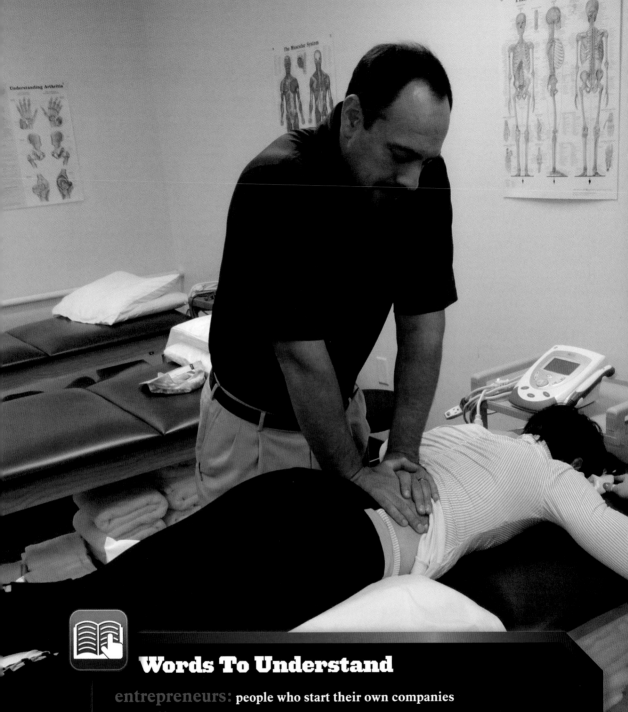

Words To Understand

entrepreneurs: people who start their own companies

on call: available to perform a service any time it's needed

outpatient: taking place outside of a hospital

workaholic: a person who works a lot

Realities of the Workplace

Working with athletes, some of them Olympic medal winners or professional champions, can seem glamorous. For sports medicine experts, though, the thrill of their job goes beyond glamour. As physical therapist Keith Steigbigel (left) says, "You wake up . . . and you're going to make someone feel better with just your hands, and that's not something everybody can say they do."

As with any job, working as a physical therapist or other sports medicine professional has some challenges that go along with rewards. Here's a look at some of those challenges.

A Long Day

For people in sports medicine, their day-to-day realities depend a lot on the setting in which they work. A PT, for example,

Therapists who work in an office usually have a regular work day with little weekend work.

could do inpatient care in a hospital and work a regular 9–5 day. Someone at an **outpatient** clinic that specializes in sports medicine, though, might have to work a little longer. Steigbigel said that on a typical day, he sees patients for eight hours, often early in the morning and later in the afternoon, then spends two hours writing reports and dealing with insurance paperwork. The pace is faster than with inpatient care, as the therapist might be overseeing several patients at once. The work can also be physically demanding, as therapists are on their feet for long stretches and sometimes have to lift patients or otherwise help them move.

Physical therapists who achieve one of the rare full-time jobs with a pro team

Trainers who work with pro sports teams have to work weekends, nights, and often seven days a week.

have long days, too. They not only work directly with injured athletes but also consult with the team's athletic trainers and strength and conditioning coaches to develop workout routines that can prevent injuries. When there is an injury, a team PT has access to all the best medical tools to speed rehabilitation and can work with the athlete daily, if necessary.

For the PT working at a clinic, the realities of the health care system are a daily concern. Both amateur athletes and some minor-league pros rely on insurance to help pay for their treatment. Many plans limit how long treatment can last and how many visits a patient can have over a year. To Steigbigel, there's no doubt that insurance restrictions are the worst part of his job.

Steigbigel said that while PTs as a whole are in demand, "You may not get your first choice [of a job] right away." But

Be Your Own Boss

A physical therapist who is not working full-time for a team might be able to set up his or her own practice. Setting up a PT clinic is like opening a small business. You need to find a good location, research the market for competing clinics, buy necessary equipment, and market yourself to find patients. You also need to understand how medical insurance payments work. Going out on your own this way can be risky, but many PTs relish the ability to control their schedules and gain the chance to make more money as an owner than as an employee.

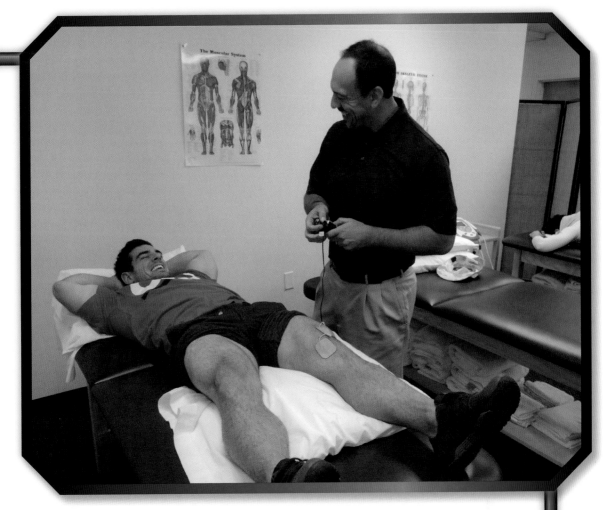

Steigbigel uses his therapy skills to aid athletes, and his people skills to bring those patients back.

therapists who want to focus on sports medicine can find jobs, and Steigbigel does not see that changing. "More and more people are participating in athletics, so there is definitely plenty of opportunity for people who want to work with athletes." Across the field, the average pay for a physical therapist in 2013 was just below $80,000.

Athletic trainers have to do their jobs in any weather. Even if the playing "field" is ice and snow for a ski race, doctors and trainers must be prepared to do their work.

Time and Weather

Long days are part of the life of athletic trainers, too. And for those working with a pro or college team, the job also forces them to work evenings and weekends. That means taking time away from families and personal interests. Bob Howard of UConn says an athletic trainer needs an understanding family that realizes what he does is not just a job, but a lifestyle. Being a bit of a **workaholic** is good for the trainer, though it can be hard on a spouse and children.

Along with the ability to balance the job's intense time requirements with personal needs, some athletic trainers need to be ready for all kinds of weather. While that's not the case for trainers who take care of indoor athletes, it's true for people like Howard or for trainers who are on the sidelines for such sports as soccer, football, or field hockey. Howard recalled game days when cold, pelting rain left his fingers and toes numb. But when an injury occurred, he had to be ready to do his job at the highest level possible.

One difficult part of an athletic trainer's job has nothing to do with treating injuries on and off the field. The trainer becomes, in a way, a member of the team, spending time with players before, during, and after practices as well as during games. When a team goes through a losing streak, the trainer shares in the sense of frustration and has to work at helping the athletes remain positive. Also hard is seeing players move on, whether through graduation or a trade, or seeing a career end because of an injury. But a trainer also has to be objective and not let his friendships get in the way of making the right decisions for the athletes' health.

Despite the challenges, competition for the top-tier athletic training jobs in college and pro sports is tough, with about 23,000 certified athletic trainers seeking about 1,200 positions at the largest universities, and even fewer positions for professional sports. High school sports, though, presents a growing field. Howard recommends that students pursuing trainer positions at any level seek out internships at colleges. Pro teams also hire interns; that was Leigh Weiss's first step in his career as an athletic trainer in the NFL. The days can be long and hot, but they provide important training—and show the students' desire to succeed in the field.

The salary for athletic trainers varies widely, given the different levels of sports they work in. The U.S. government said the national average in 2013 was about $45,000, but some earn more than $66,000.

Long Training, High Pay

For sports doctors and surgeons, one of the hardest parts of their job comes before they ever treat an injured athlete. Becoming a medical doctor requires some of the most intense educational preparation of any field. The typical residency, which comes after medical school, lasts from three to seven years. Residents spend long hours at hospitals, seeing patients and further developing their skills. There are certificates for sports medicine and sports

In baseball's minor leagues, the medical service is professional, even if the pay is not major league.

orthopedic surgery. Once certified, doctors must stay current in their field, since they have to renew their certification every six to ten years.

As with other jobs in sports medicine, landing a job with a pro or top college team is not easy. But primary care sports doctors can also set up their own practices or work with a group of doctors. Sports doctors and surgeons make more than any other

Sports psychologists can make a good living helping athletes deal with success and failure.

professionals involved in sports medicine. The average salaries range between $180,000 and $233,000. And while competition to work for a sports team is high, there is a growing demand for primary care sports doctors outside of organized athletics.

A Life of the Mind

For sports psychologists, the training is rigorous as well, though not as hard as for medical doctors. And competition is tough, though the field is growing. The American Psychological Association (APA) estimated in 2012 that about 20 top universities hired their own psychologists for their athletes, while up to 100 more worked with outside sports psychologists. Pro teams also sometimes bring in psychologists as needed. Positions are also available with individual athletes. Some parents are hiring psychologists to help their children do better in sports.

Sports psychologists often open their own practice and seek out a variety of clients. Dr. Charlie Brown opened a company called Get Your Head in the Game, and he sees artistic performers and business leaders as well as athletes. The skills he uses to help athletes apply to anyone who faces pressure, especially in competitive situations. Dr. Sean Richardson told Careers in Psychology that sports psychologists might spend almost all of their time working with athletes for a while, then find that work drops off and they need to seek other clients. They need to be **entrepreneurs**, Richardson said. "If you hope to go look at a job board and get your dream career, that just probably won't happen in this field."

For the psychologists who do end up working for a team, the issue of time management arises. Traveling with a team or having to be **on call** can cut into their own time for family or relaxation.

As with other positions in sports medicine, the salaries for psychologists can vary widely. Working at a university, they might earn between $60,000 and $100,000. In a private practice, the salary depends on how many clients the doctor can attract and how much those clients can afford to pay.

Whether you choose to become a physical therapist, sports doctor, or sports psychologist, you will have the chance to be part of what you are passionate about: sports. But you have to make sure you consider that just because you are part of the sports world, does not mean that it's all fun and games. Especially for people in health careers in sports, the pressure can be significant. Athletes want to get back on the field, while team managers can put pressure on medical people to do their work faster. It's an important part of your job as the health professional to put the needs of the athlete—your patient—above the needs of the team. Once you put on the coat of a health professional, you leave your cap with your favorite team logo behind.

Text-Dependent Questions

1. Is the average pay of a physical therapist more or less than $100,000?

2. How long is a typical residency for a person training to be a doctor?

3. What does Keith Steigbigel say is "the worst part" of his job?

Research Project

Using Internet research, make a chart of the average salaries in your state for the jobs featured in this chapter: athletic trainer, physical therapist, sports medicine physician, and sports psychologist.

Words To Understand

arthroscopic: relating to an arthroscope, a device used for some surgeries

incision: a cut made during some medical procedures

ligament: a tissue that connects bones near a joint

The Nitty-Gritty

CHAPTER 4

When a Chicago Blackhawks player goes down hard on the ice, orthopedic surgeon Michael Terry (left) is usually there to see it. Terry goes to most of the National Hockey League team's games, sitting behind the bench ready to offer his help. Along with on-the-scene diagnoses of concussions and treatment of cuts, Terry performs operations on the players.

The years of training sports physicians undergo lets them perform a range of health services for athletes. For Terry, one of those procedures is **arthroscopic** surgery. For another team doctor on the field or in the locker room, it might mean popping a dislocated joint back into place. While all sports medicine professionals offer care, both preventive and after an injury, the specifics of what each does defines their job. Here's a more detailed look at just some of those specific tasks.

Hands-on Work

While physical therapists can have patients work with weights and elastic bands and treat them with ice packs and electrical stimulations, the therapists' work begins with their own eyes and hands. Assessing the extent of a joint injury begins with

Elastic bands can help injured muscles stretch without using heavy weights.

watching the patient try to do routine activities that involve the affected body part. With athletes, that can mean watching them walk or bend or make throwing or kicking movements to see how much the movement varies from what's considered normal.

The next step is to have the patients sit on an examining table so the therapist can move the body part in all directions. This process is part of determining the range of motion. Through it the therapist can determine how the tissue around the joint feels as the joint reaches the normal end of its range of motion. When there's a problem reaching this "end range," the therapist first has to help the patient regain that movement before restoring full strength and full function. The therapist's knowledge of physiology and kinesiology all come into play here, as well as the experience gained through clinical work while in school.

It's a Wrap

For athletic trainers, much of their job is hands-on, too. One of the most important tasks is one that many sports fans might overlook, but which athletes appreciate—taping up various body parts that come under strain during a game. To Bob Howard, taping an ankle, for example, is easy, something he has perfected with years of practice. Yet, he says, "People are in awe of that."

Taping any joint requires using the right kind of tape, starting with pre-wrap, which goes over all the skin. This tape is not sticky, and it provides some padding and protection from the adhesive athletic tape that provides the main support.

To wrap an ankle, for example, the next step would be to put several strips of athletic tape at the top of the wrapping to anchor the pre-wrap, then place several strips down the inside of the leg, around the heel and up the other side. The trainers know from their study of the human body and the nature of sports injuries that those wraps help stabilize the **ligament** and prevent sprains.

The next step involves wrapping around the leg and then down around the heel, working the tape on both sides and putting on three layers. The trainers learn not to tape so low on the foot that it covers the bone of the pinky toe, as that can make the toe more likely to break. Taping is as much an art as a science.

A Healing Cut

When surgery is called for, a sports orthopedic surgeon, like Michael Terry of the Chicago Blackhawks, takes over. While Terry performs all sorts of medical services for the team—even acting as the family physician for a player just traded to the Blackhawks—his specialty is surgery. And for repairing torn tendons and ligaments, Terry and other sports surgeons rely on a procedure called arthroscopy.

The process begins with the surgeon making a small **incision** near the injured joint, then moving thin, pencil-shaped devices into the area. The arthroscope has a light and a tiny

Sports surgeons operate on patients in hospital settings. Many modern surgeries use cameras to look inside the patient as they work; doctors here are watching the screen in the background.

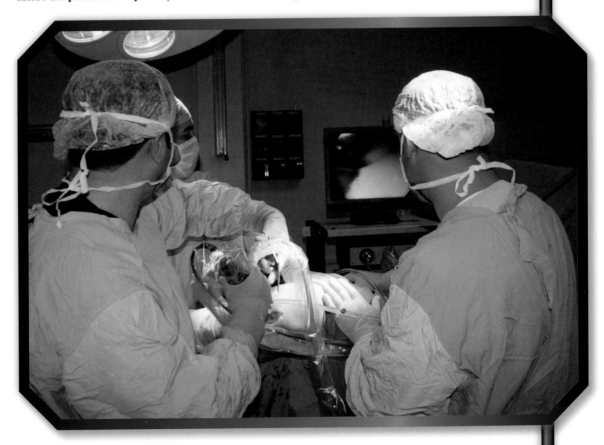

camera, which transmits images of the injured area to a TV screen the surgeon can see. The main benefit of this procedure is that it gives the doctor detailed information about the injury without performing major surgery. If he sees a repair is needed, the surgeon makes additional small cuts to insert surgical tools. The small cuts mean the patient recovers faster.

For someone like Dr. Terry, who sees patients in a hospital in addition to his work for the Blackhawks, one of the benefits of the job is seeing a wide range of patients and injuries. He told a Northwestern University news site, "I find myself doing hip surgery on a sixty-year-old one day and a knee procedure on a teenager the next." But once the patient is on the table, he said, it doesn't matter if he or she is a weekend warrior or a star player for the Blackhawks. The focus is on treating the joint in front of him.

Getting the Mental Edge

When working with athletes, sports psychologists have several useful techniques. They teach them to the athletes so they can use the techniques on their own during training and competition. One of the most important tools is imagery or visualization. The psychologists teach the athletes to imagine every aspect of what a game or event might be like. For a skier, for example, that might mean feeling the cold air, hearing the cheering crowds, and imagining going down the slope with speed and precision. In some cases, the athletes actually move their arms and legs as they would during their event, while simply standing in their room or waiting in a line. Olympic skier Emily Cook told *The New York Times,* "We're all up there flapping our arms. It looks insane, but it works."

Imagery techniques are not just for competition. Sports psychologists sometimes have athletes imagine seeing a broken bone or other injury heal. They might also help the athletes deal with the fear of failure. After working with sports psychologist Nicole Detling, Cook developed an image to help overcome fear. She imagined her fear as a big red balloon, which in her mind she popped with a pin.

Sports psychologists also give athletes techniques for relaxing before an event. These can include deep-breathing exercises and progressive relaxation. Sports psychologist JoAnn Dahlkoetter also encourages athletes to stay focused on the present moment, whether during training or a competition. As she wrote in the Huffington Post, "Instead of replaying past mistakes, or worrying about the future, let past and future events fade into the background. Be right on, right here, right now...."

Breathe out unwanted thoughts with your next exhale and refocus your attention instantly on what is important right now, at this moment."

Choosing the Path for You

As you've seen throughout this book, sports medicine professionals help athletes of all sorts in a variety of ways. While the educational requirements can be tough, the experts across the various fields covered here all stress how great the rewards are. Physical therapist Keith Steigbigel said PTs taking care of injured people is an "invaluable skill." Getting the job you want in the field, said athletic trainer Bob Howard, means you have to "go full steam. Do every little extra to make yourself good." For Dr. Sean Richardson, a career in his field means having a desire, getting the right education, and making connections with people in the field. Then satisfaction will come, as he told Careers in Psychology, after you help an athlete make the mental changes that lead to a "change on the field and [they] become even better in sports..."

Sports medicine is a profession for people who love the thrill of competition and want to help others.

Helping athletes gain the mental focus to succeed is the goal of the sports pyschologist.

Text-Dependent Questions

1. For what team is Michael Terry the team physician?

2. What skill does Bob Howard describe as a key part of the athletic trainer's art?

3. How does arthroscopic surgery differ from regular surgery?

Research Project

Now that you've read about some major areas of sports medicine, write down three pluses and minuses, in your opinion, for you trying out each of the four main areas: athletic trainer, physical therapist, sports surgeon, and sports psychologist.

Find Out More

Books

Badasch, Shirley A. and Doreen S. Chesebro. *Health Science Fundamentals: Exploring Career Pathways.* Upper Saddle River, NJ: Pearson Learning Solutions, 2011.

Kamberg, Mary-Lane. *A Career As an Athletic Trainer.* New York: Rosen Publishing, 2013.

Kummer, Patricia A. *Sports Medicine Doctor.* Ann Arbor, MI: Cherry Lake Publishing, 2009

Web Sites

American College of Sports Medicine
/www.acsm.org/

American Physical Therapy Association
www.apta.org/

Explore Health Careers
explorehealthcareers.org/en/home

National Athletic Trainers' Association
www.nata.org/

Series Glossary of Key Terms

academic: relating to classes and studies

alumni: people who graduate from a particular college

boilerplate: a standard set of text and information that an organization puts at the end of every press release

compliance: the action of following rules

conferences: groups of schools in which schools within a group play each other frequently in sports

constituencies: a specific group of people related by their connection to an organization or demographic group

credential: a document that gives the holder permission to take part in an event in a way not open to the public

eligibility: a student's ability to compete in sports, based on grades or other school or NCAA requirements

entrepreneurs: people who start their own companies

freelance: a person who does not work full-time for a company, but is paid for each piece of work

gamer: in sports journalism, a write-up of a game

intercollegiate: something that takes places between two schools, such as a sporting event

internships: positions that rarely offer pay but provide on-the-job experience

orthopedics: the branch of medicine that specializes in preventing and correcting problems with bones and muscles

objective: material written based solely on the facts of a situation

recruiting: the process of finding the best athletes to play for a team

revenue: money earned from a business or event

spreadsheets: computer programs that calculates numbers and organizes information in rows and columns

subjective: material written from a particular point of view, choosing facts to suit the opinion

Index

Credits

About the Author

Michael Burgan has written more than 250 books for children and teens, as well as newspaper articles and blog posts. Although not an athlete, he has written on amateur and professional sports, including books on the Basketball Hall of Fame, the Olympics, and great moments in baseball. And although not a medical professional, he regularly writes Web content on a variety of health topics. He lives in Santa Fe, New Mexico.